Nature's Changes

CAMOUFLAGE
CHANGING TO HIDE

Bobbie Kalman

🌳 Crabtree Publishing Company

www.crabtreebooks.com

Created by Bobbie Kalman

For my mother, Valerie, on her 80th birthday.
I love you, Mom. You're the best!

Author and Editor-in-Chief
Bobbie Kalman

Substantive editor
Kathryn Smithyman

Editors
Molly Aloian
Kelley MacAulay
Reagan Miller

Research
Niki Walker

Design
Margaret Amy Reiach
Samantha Crabtree (cover)
Robert MacGregor (series logo)

Production coordinator
Katherine Kantor

Photo research
Crystal Foxton

Consultant
Patricia Loesche, Ph.D., Animal Behavior Program,
Department of Psychology, University of Washington

Illustrations
Barbara Bedell: pages 16, 24
Margaret Amy Reiach: series logo illustrations,
    pages 10, 23, 25

Photographs
Bobbie Kalman: page 17 (top)
Visuals Unlimited: Tom Walker: page 28 (bottom)
Other images by Corbis, Corel, Creatas, Digital Stock,
    Digital Vision, Otto Rogge Photography, and Photodisc

Crabtree Publishing Company

www.crabtreebooks.com   1-800-387-7650

Copyright © **2005 CRABTREE PUBLISHING COMPANY.**
All rights reserved. No part of this publication may be
reproduced, stored in a retrieval system or be transmitted in
any form or by any means, electronic, mechanical, photocopying,
recording, or otherwise, without the prior written permission
of Crabtree Publishing Company. In Canada: We acknowledge the
financial support of the Government of Canada through the Book
Publishing Industry Development Program (BPIDP) for our
publishing activities.

Cataloging-in-Publication Data
Kalman, Bobbie.
  Camouflage : changing to hide / Bobbie Kalman.
    p. cm. -- (Nature's changes series)
  Includes index.
  ISBN-13: 978-0-7787-2272-4 (RLB)
  ISBN-10: 0-7787-2272-4 (RLB)
  ISBN-13: 978-0-7787-2306-6 (pbk.)
  ISBN-10: 0-7787-2306-2 (pbk.)
  1. Camouflage (Biology)--Juvenile literature. I. Title. II. Series.
  QL767.K35 2005
  591.47'2--dc22
                                    2005000490
                                    LC

**Published in
the United States**
PMB16A
350 Fifth Ave.
Suite 3308
New York, NY
10118

**Published
in Canada**
616 Welland Ave.,
St. Catharines, Ontario
Canada
L2M 5V6

**Published in the
United Kingdom**
73 Lime Walk
Headington
Oxford
OX3 7AD
United Kingdom

**Published
in Australia**
386 Mt. Alexander Rd.,
Ascot Vale (Melbourne)
VIC 3032

Contents

What is camouflage?

The leaf-tailed gecko shown below is **camouflaged** against the tree bark underneath its body. To be camouflaged means to be hidden. Animals with camouflage have colors, patterns, or **textures** on their bodies that match their surroundings. The colors, patterns, and textures of this gecko's body match the tree bark almost exactly!

4

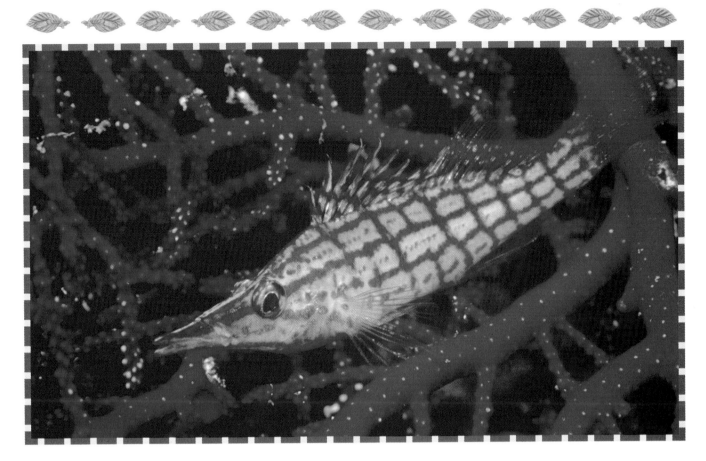

Patterns and textures

The hawkfish in the picture above blends in with the **corals** that surround it. The patterns on the fish's body look like the shapes made by the corals around the fish. The grasshopper on the right is camouflaged by its color and the texture of its skin. Its color blends in with stones, and the bumps on its skin look like bits of soil.

Shapes that fool

Some animals are hidden because they **mimic**, or imitate, parts of their surroundings. This kind of camouflage is called **mimicry**. Animals may mimic rocks, twigs, or leaves. Animals that use mimicry are often the hardest to see. The colors and shapes of these animals **disguise** them perfectly!

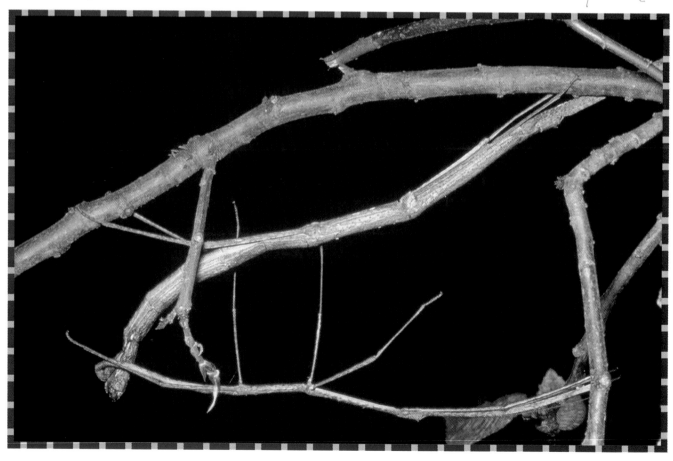

Can you see the two stick insects in this picture? They look just like tree branches!

Not what they seem

Animals have mimicry to look like things they are not. The stinkbug above is the same color and shape as the leaf underneath it. When the bug stays still, other animals may not see it. The fly on the right looks just like a wasp that stings. Even though the fly cannot sting, animals might stay away from it because they are afraid of getting stung!

7

Why do animals hide?

Animals hide to stay alive. Some animals hide so they will not be eaten. Other animals hide so they can catch food. Animals that hunt other animals for food are called **predators**.

The animals predators eat are called **prey**. Both predators and prey can have camouflaged bodies. Prey are camouflaged so that predators will have trouble seeing them.

This fish is camouflaged from predators. It blends in with the corals around it.

8

Predators hide, too

Predators do not use camouflage to protect themselves. They use camouflage to hide so they can get close to their prey. The closer they get, the better their chances are of catching food!

This green insect is a praying mantis. It is a predator. It hides among green plants and waits for other insects to crawl or fly close enough to catch. This fly did not see the praying mantis and got caught!

Hiding the babies, too

Animal babies need camouflage, too. Most babies are small and weak, and they move slowly. It is easy for predators to catch them. Having camouflaged bodies helps baby animals hide from predators.

Green-sea-turtle babies have soft shells, so they are easily eaten by many predators. The green bodies of the turtles blend in with the seaweed on which the turtles feed. Being camouflaged helps the baby turtles hide from birds and other predators.

10

Staying safe

Some animal mothers try to keep predators away from their babies. Babies still need camouflage, even if their mothers protect them. They need camouflage so that predators will not see the babies while their mothers are away hunting.

The baby cougars above have spots that help them hide in the shadows of trees.

Baby seals are white because they spend most of their time on snow and ice.

Where do they hide?

An animal's camouflage blends in with its **habitat**. A habitat is an animal's natural home. Forests, deserts, **wetlands**, and **coral reefs** are habitats. Each habitat is made up of different shapes and colors. Animals hide by matching parts of their habitats.

Most forests have green trees with brown trunks. Deserts are mainly brown. Some wetlands have dark waters with green or brown plants growing in them. Coral reefs are ocean habitats that contain many shapes and colors!

The colors and patterns of this horned frog match the colors and patterns of its wetland habitat.

This collared lizard is brown like its desert habitat. The textures and shapes of the scales on its body look like the shapes of the plants that grow in deserts.

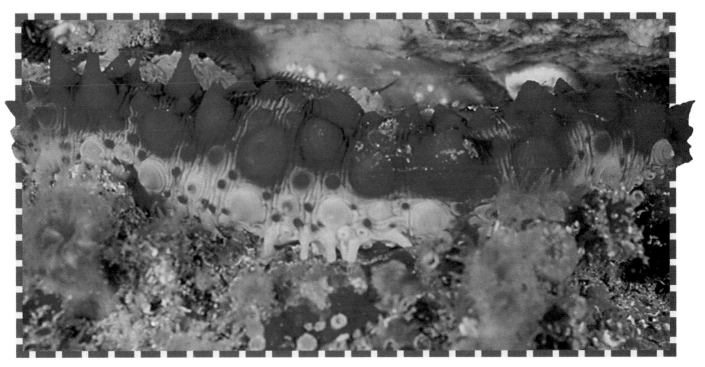

This sea cucumber is a brightly colored animal. It blends in with its colorful coral reef habitat.

One main color

Many animals need only one color to camouflage them. Their fur, skin, or feathers are almost the same colors as the leaves, sand, or rocks in their habitats.

Many forest animals are green or brown. Lizards, snakes, and insects often match the colors of forest plants. The caterpillar above is green, just like the leaves on which it lives and feeds.

The color of soil

Animals that live on the ground are often brown. This prairie dog's fur is the same color as the soil in its desert habitat. Having brown fur helps camouflage prairie dogs.

Dark and light

The back of the bird is dark.

The belly of the bird is white.

Some animals spend most of their time under water or in the air. These animals need a special type of camouflage to help them blend in. This type of camouflage is called **countershading**. Animals with countershading have dark backs and light bellies. Many birds and sea animals have countershading.

Many seabirds have white bellies. Having white bellies helps these birds catch fish. The fish that swim in the water below may not see the birds swooping down to grab them.

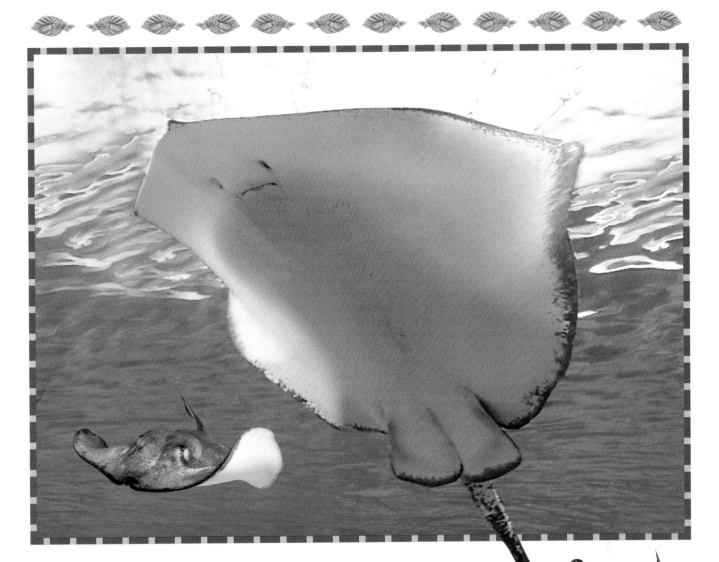

How does countershading work?

A stingray has a white belly and a dark back. When a predator or a prey animal swims above the stingray, the animal may not see the stingray because its dark gray back blends in with the dark floor of the ocean. When a predator or a prey animal swims below the stingray, the animal may not see the stingray because its white belly blends in with the bright, sunlit surface of the water.

Spots and stripes

Some animals are covered with spots. Spots can blend in with small stones or with the patterns on rocks. In forests, spots help camouflage animals, such as the baby deer shown below. The deer's spotted coat helps hide the animal on the forest floor. The spots look just like the rays of sunlight that shine through the leaves of trees.

leopard gecko

When the deer is lying still, its spots blend in with the sunspots and shadows in the forest. The spots help hide the young deer from predators.

Confusing predators

Some animals are covered with stripes. An animal's stripes help confuse predators. Stripes hide the **outline**, or shape, of an animal's body. Predators may not be able to tell where the animal's body begins or ends, so they may not know where to attack.

Group protection

Some striped animals, such as these angelfish, stay safe in groups. Their stripes help them blend in with one another. To a predator such as a shark or a dolphin, these fish may look like one huge animal! A predator might not attack an animal that seems larger than itself.

19

Where are the eyes?

Some animals have stripes over their eyes. The stripes hide the eyes of the animals. A predator often kills an animal by attacking its head.

If a predator cannot see the eyes of its prey, it may not attack the prey's head. Having a stripe that hides its eyes might save an animal's life!

Heads or tails?

Some animals, such as butterfly fish, have spots on their tails. These spots are called **eyespots** because they look like large eyes. Eyespots cause a predator to attack an animal's tail instead of its head. When an animal with an eyespot sees a predator coming toward its tail, it might have time to get away!

eyespot

Spots on wings

Some moths and butterflies have eyespots on their wings. Eyespots on wings look like the eyes of large animals. When a predator sees large "eyes" on a moth or a butterfly, it may not attack its prey.

This butterfly fish has eyespots. Its real eyes are hidden by stripes.

This moth has four eyespots on its wings. Two of the moth's eyespots look quite large. When the moth sees a predator, it opens its wings. When the predator sees the moth's large eyespots, it might mistake the moth for a large animal and leave it alone!

Can you see them?

The shrimp in the picture above is hard to see because its body is **transparent**, or see-through. Predators may not see transparent animals because the colors around them show through their bodies and make the animals almost disappear.

Almost invisible

In the picture below, part of the
fish's body is transparent. The fish
is almost invisible against the coral
around it. The frog on the right is
called a glass frog. Why do you
think it was given this name?

Quick changes

sea horse

In the blink of an eye, some animals, such as octopuses, sea horses, and cuttlefish, are able to change the way their bodies look. These animals can change the colors and patterns on their bodies to match the colors and patterns in different parts of their habitats.

cuttlefish

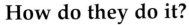

How do they do it?

Animals that can change color have skin **cells** that contain **pigments**. Pigments are natural substances that give plants or animals their colors. When octopuses move from place to place, they change the amount of pigment in their cells. Changing the amount of pigment makes their skin change color, so the animals always blend in with their habitats. Not only can octopuses change color, they can also make their skin look bumpy or smooth!

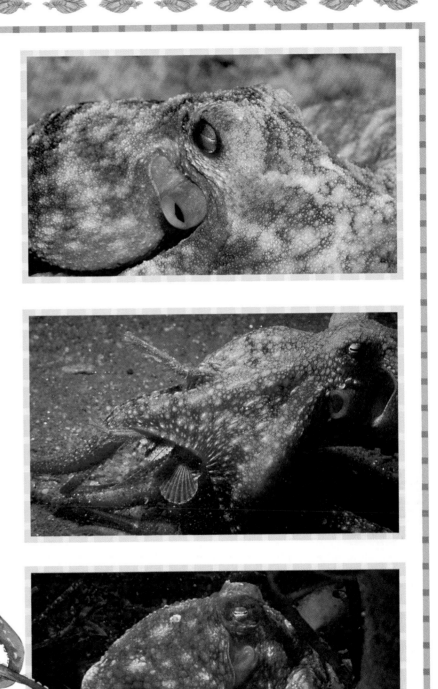

Color-changing lizards

Many lizards can change color to match the colors of their surroundings. Lizards have colored cells in their skin. The colors include yellow, blue, and red. To change color, lizards make the cells larger or smaller. The skin of the green anole below can change from green to brown or show both green and brown at once.

This double-crested basilisk has changed color to match some of the colors in the tree it is climbing. Which of its colors match the tree?

Showing how they feel

Chameleons are the most famous color-changers of all! Chameleons change color in the same way that other lizards do, but they do not change color to hide. They change color to show other animals that they are angry or afraid.

Changing coats

Many places have cold winters and mild summers. In winter, these habitats are covered with white snow and ice. In summer, the ground is gray and brown.

New season, new color

The colors of the fur or feathers of some animals are different in the different seasons. Twice a year, the colors change. Animals **molt**, or shed, their fur or feathers. In winter, they have white feathers or fur so their bodies will blend in with the snow. In summer, their fur or feathers are mostly brown or gray, to match the summer colors of their habitats.

(top) In summer, willow ptarmigans have brown feathers.
(bottom) In winter, the feathers of willow ptarmigans are white.

Arctic foxes have thick white fur that keeps them warm during the freezing winter months in the Arctic. The white fur blends in with the winter ice and snow. In spring, the fur of arctic foxes turns grayish brown.

The young arctic fox, shown left, was born in spring. Its fur matches the summer colors of the Arctic. The young fox will shed its gray fur before winter and grow a thick white coat, just like the coat of the fox above.

How are they hiding?

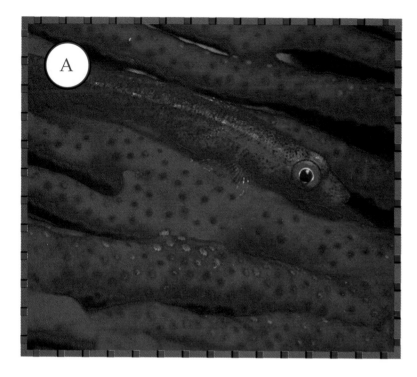

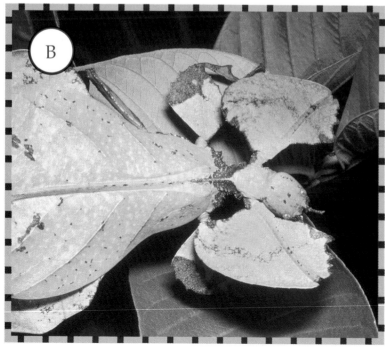

Different animals are camouflaged in different ways. Each of the pictures on these two pages shows a type of camouflage. Read the questions below and find the picture that goes with each question. The answers are on page 31.

Which is it?

1. Which animal is using one color to hide itself?

2. Which animal uses mimicry to hide?

3. Which animal's shape blends in with the shapes in its habitat?

4. Which animal changes its coat to blend in with the colors of the seasons?

5. Which animal is able to change color in seconds?

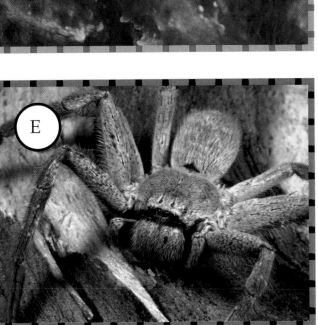

Hidden in different ways:

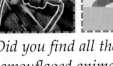

Did you find all the camouflaged animals?

Answers:

1. E The wolf spider uses one color to hide itself.

2. B The leaf insect uses mimicry. Its body looks like the leaves on which the insect lives and feeds.

3. A The goby's shape matches the shapes in the fish's habitat.

4. D The arctic wolf changes color with the seasons. Its coat is white in winter and gray in summer.

5. C Octopuses change color quickly when they move to different parts of their habitats.

31

Words to know

Note: Boldfaced words that are defined in the text may not appear in the glossary.

cell The most basic part of every living thing; most plants and animals are made of millions of cells

coral reef A large rocklike structure found in oceans, which is formed by millions of coral skeletons piling up on top of one another

corals Small animals that live in oceans and stay in only one place

disguise To change the way one looks to look like something else

habitat The natural place where a plant or an animal lives

outline The line that shows the shape or outer edge of something

texture The look and feel of the surface of something; how rough or smooth a surface is

wetland An area of land that is under shallow water some or all of the time

Index

1 2 3 4 5 6 7 8 9 0   Printed in the U.S.A.   4 3 2 1 0 9 8 7 6 5